An Action Guide to Put the C in PLC

REFLECTING AND DOING

An Action Guide to Put the C in PLC

in PLC

REFLECTING AND DOING

Chad Dumas, Ed.D.

Copyright © 2021 by Chad Dumas

All rights reserved under the Pan-American and International Copyright Conventions. This book may not be reproduced, in whole or in part, in any form or by any means, electronic or mechanical, including photocopying, recording, or by any information storage and retrieval system now known or hereafter invented, without written permission from the publisher.

Published by Next Learning Solutions Press
www.nextlearningsolutionspress.com

ISBN (paperback): 978-1-7357462-2-7

Edited by David Aretha
Cover and interior design by Christy Collins, Constellation Book Services

Printed in the United States of America

CONTENTS

PREFACE   *vii*

Introduction   1
Chapter One: Charismatic Leadership ≠ Success   5
Chapter Two: Team Staff   21
Chapter Three: Staff Meetings   33
Chapter Four: Principles of Adult Learning   41
Chapter Five: Continuous Improvement and Innovation   53
Chapter Six: Model Learning   67
Chapter Seven: Allocate Resources   79
Chapter Eight: Involve Staff   93
Chapter Nine: Principles of Student Learning   105
Chapter Ten: Principles of Change and Sustainability   125
Chapter Eleven: A Call to Action   137

Appendix   *141*

PREFACE

In the process of writing *Let's Put the C in PLC: A Practical Guide for School Leaders*, my publishing guide, Martha Bullen, suggested that I think about writing a workbook to assist school leaders with translating their knowledge into practice. The more I thought about it, the more excited I became: Our work is not just about knowing; it is about doing. The book is a great starting place to increase your knowledge, and this supplemental resource will be a useful tool to help bridge that knowing-doing gap and change your practice.

Within short order, I started on this action guide. Concepts from the *Let's Put the C in PLC* are presented, without much elaboration and minus the stories or additional resources. Instead, the concepts are accompanied by questions to reflect on and practical exercises to assist you in putting the C in your Professional Learning Community.

Improving your practice begins with knowledge. And though this action guide is not a substitute for the book, I hope it will assist you in translating what is written and understood into practice and, ultimately, habits. I hope you use it individually, and also engage with others to challenge your thinking and practices. Indeed, you will gain more from this action guide by engaging with others in these activities to learn from and with each other.

While it may not be typical to have practices in the preface, I think it's important for these concepts to become part of who you are. To make it easier for group study, items are labeled with the part of the book followed by a letter for the sequence of item. So P.a. is Preface question a. Intro.a is the first item in the Introduction. I.a. is the first item in Chapter One. And Challenge Questions are also identified in a similar sequence.

Let's begin!

In the text, I make this assertion:

Professional learning community works.
Principals are the key to making it happen.
Is there a knowing-doing gap?

Question P.a.

Do you agree with this assertion? Why or why not?

Question P.b.

What examples (personal or professional) of a knowing-doing gap exist in your life?

Question P.c.

What have been some strategies and actions that you have taken to close those gaps?

Question P.d.

What have been some of the successes and pitfalls you have encountered in those previous experiences?

Question P.e.

What about those experiences can you apply to the learning in this book?

"When people know better, they do better."
—*Maya Angelou*

The Ten Elements of Principal Knowledge (Dumas, 2010) for creating a collaborative workplace environment for teachers are:

1. Recognize that charismatic leadership does not equal success.
2. Team teachers for effectiveness.
3. Focus staff meetings on student learning.
4. Use principles of adult learning.
5. Apply elements of continuous improvement and innovation.
6. Model your own professional learning.
7. Allocate resources.
8. Involve staff in important decisions.
9. Understand principles of student learning.
10. Utilize principles of change and sustainability.

Question P.f.

If you were to sort these ten elements into three "piles" based on how IMPORTANT they are to you, your learning, and your organization, how might you do that? What themes emerge?

IMPORTANT	MORE IMPORTANT	MOST IMPORTANT

Question P.g.

Group these ten elements into three "piles" based on how URGENT they are to you, your learning, and your organization. What do you notice?

LESS URGENT	URGENT	MOST URGENT

Question P.h.

Based on these prioritizations, what are some strategies you might use to ensure that you honor this thinking in your study and improvement?

INTRODUCTION

This workbook is not a replacement for *Let's Put the C in PLC*. It is intended to be used alongside the text with questions to push your thinking, challenges to examine your practice, and prompts to engage with others in implementing the concepts that are found therein. It also has practical challenges that, if you complete them, will help you implement your learning.

By using this action guide, you will translate the new declarative knowledge from the book into your daily practice. There are some short excerpts from the book, but mostly it has questions and exercises to dig deeper into your own thinking and provide you with new insights to explore. Questions are purely reflective for you to consider, whereas Challenge Exercises are those that you will use to engage with others. And at the end of each chapter there are a couple of pages open for your notes and reflections.

Question Intro.a.

In the book I state that "Top-down approaches not only won't work, Jim Knight goes even further to state that the top-down model of leadership often guarantees failure in professional organizations and communities. This has been tried, and each time it fails. What is needed is a change of heart, a change of culture, and with it, changes in practice. We need to create communities where learning for all thrives. Learning for students. Learning for staff. Learning for administrators."

What are some examples of top-down initiatives that you have experienced? What are some examples of top-down initiatives that you have led?

Question Intro.b.

What were some of the short- and long-term outcomes (good and bad) of these?

Question Intro.c.

What changes could have been made to how these initiatives were led and implemented so that they became embedded in the culture of the organization?

Question Intro.d.

What are some current and/or future initiatives that you will be leading? What about your prior experiences will help ensure that the changes lead to the desired results?

Question Intro.e.

How will creating a collaborative environment for teachers be helpful in ensuring the success of these changes?

CHAPTER ONE
CHARISMATIC LEADERSHIP ≠ SUCCESS

Elements of Principal Knowledge in Creating a Collaborative Workplace Environment for Teachers

To build a collaborative culture of professional learning, principals know and understand that:

1. Charismatic leadership is not necessary for long-term success
    A. Relationships ARE necessary for long-term success
    B. Personal Clarity
    C. Dialogue
    D. Rapport
    E. Pause
    F. Paraphrase
    G. Prompt

Charisma ≠ Success

Question 1.a.

On a scale of 1 to 10, how charismatic do you think you are?

1	2	3	4	5	6	7	8	9	10
NOT AT ALL									HIGHLY CHARISMATIC

Question 1.b.

Given your score, what considerations do you need to think about to improve your practice and organization? In what ways might you use your level of charisma to the advantage of your organization?

Question 1.c.

The book provides the following quotes:

Leadership is not a solo act. In the thousands of personal-best leadership cases we studied, we have yet to encounter a single example of extraordinary achievement that occurred without the active involvement and support of many people. Fostering collaboration is the route to high performance.

School leadership is a team sport.

In your experience, what are some examples that would prove these quotes true, as well as non-examples that might call the veracity of these claims into question?

Question 1.d.

Collins (2001) states that leaders with a combination of profound humility and intense professional will lead to lasting greatness. In what ways do you personally demonstrate these two qualities? Be specific.

Question 1.e.

What are some actionable steps you can take to become more humble and exhibit intense professional will?

CHALLENGE EXERCISE 1.a.

You previously rated yourself on your personal level of charisma. Now ask others to (anonymously) rate you. What differences emerge? How might this inform your leadership?

CHALLENGE EXERCISE 1.b.

Think of an upcoming meeting that you will attend where you are a senior member of the group. What strategies might you use to ensure that you are last (or close to last) in offering your own thoughts?

CHALLENGE EXERCISE 1.c.

At an upcoming meeting where you are a senior member of the group, take 3 x 5 cards with you. At the conclusion of the meeting, ask each participant to write down feedback for you based on this question: In what ways might I behave differently for you to better know that I am just one member of the team?

CHALLENGE EXERCISE 1.d.

Great leaders lead by example—they walk their talk. Rate yourself on a 1 to 10 scale on your ability to do this. Then, at a future meeting with staff, ask staff to (anonymously) rate you on a sticky note on this scale, together with any additional feedback. Use this data to inform your next steps.

Question 1.f.

> **Relationships are founded upon clarity of language, goals, and actions.**

Rate your own ability to remember your staff's names and interests. What are some strategies you might use or resources you might access in order to increase this skill?

Question 1.g.

Clarity: Dennis Sparks contends that deep and meaningful relationships are based upon personal clarity about who you are, where you are going, and how you will get there.

Reflect on your personal clarity in these three areas.

Who are you?

Where are you going (i.e., personal and professional goals)?

What are key steps that you are taking to get there?

Question 1.h.

What are some actions you might take to become clearer about who you are, where you are going, and how you will get there? What role does your language (including choice, what you say, and how you say it) play in communicating this to others?

CHALLENGE EXERCISE 1.e.

Informally, in one-on-one situations, ask staff and colleagues this question: Who do you perceive me, as a leader, to be? What do I do and say that communicates this to you and others? Use this data to guide your next steps.

Question 1.i.

What goals do you have for yourself? Your school? If they are not stretch goals, what might you do to make them such?

Question 1.j.

What actions are you taking to achieve these goals? What are additional actions that you might take? Remember, "getting a good idea begins with getting your hands on many ideas." From whom and when might you access to get additional ideas?

Question 1.k.

Dialogue: Freire contends that dialogue is "an act of creation" and that "without dialogue there is no communication, and without communication, there can be no true education." Using his principles, reflect on the extent to which each of these is part of who you are as a person and a leader.

Love

Humility

Faith

Trust

Hope

Critical Thinking

CHALLENGE EXERCISE 1.f.

Write the six principles of effective dialogue, noted above, on a 3 x 5 notecard. Take this card with you to meetings, and prior to entering, take the card out and consider which one you want to really focus on for that meeting. At the conclusion, reflect on how you did. Write down those reflections.

> **"Listening is only powerful and effective if it is authentic. Authenticity means that you are listening because you are curious and because you care, not just because you are supposed to. The issue, then, is this: Are you curious? Do you care?"**
>
> *Stone et al. 1999*

Three + One

CHALLENGE EXERCISE 1.g.

With family and friends, notice your physical rapport with them. Take actions to "test" and see if they follow you. Have fun with it. Notice when you are not in rapport with someone and work to get there.

CHALLENGE EXERCISE 1.h.

Be intentional about pausing after people speak. Devise a strategy to ensure that you do this (e.g., count to three, take a deep breath, look off into the distance for a moment to think, etc).

CHALLENGE EXERCISE 1.i.

With friends or family, practice paraphrasing when you are in low-risk situations. Ask them for feedback. Continue to refine this skill so that it becomes natural and a part of who you are in all conversations—both low- and high-risk.

CHALLENGE EXERCISE 1.j.

Reflect on a recent interaction where asking questions was or would have been a useful tactic to build the relationship. What worked? What didn't work? What can you do next time to ensure greater success? How can you remind yourself to do these things in the moment?

CHALLENGE EXERCISE 1.k.

Consider how you might take the learning from this chapter and apply it to a remote environment. For the most part you will find identical applications—however, there may be a few times or places where there are unique considerations. What specific challenges does the remote environment have in relation to this chapter? How can you leverage these challenges to work for you?

CHALLENGE EXERCISE 1.l.

Go to the Thinking Collaborative website (www.thinkingcollaborative.com). Identify three resources or tools that might be helpful to improve your own practice as a collaborator, inquirer, and leader in the next couple of weeks. Commit to using and reflecting on them.

NOTES AND REFLECTIONS

CHAPTER TWO
TEAM STAFF

Elements of Principal Knowledge in Creating a Collaborative Workplace Environment for Teachers

To build a collaborative culture of professional learning, principals know and understand that:

2. Teachers should work in teams. Effective elements include:
   A. Effective grouping
   B. A focus on improving instruction/teaching each other by:
      1. Working, planning, and thinking together
      2. Reflecting via dialogue re: professional issues
      3. Observing and reacting to teaching, curriculum, and assessment
      4. Joint lesson planning and curriculum development
   C. The use of protocols
   D. The training of teachers in the skills and knowledge to collaborate
   E. An incentive system
   F. The deprivatization of the classroom
   G. Networking with teachers in other buildings

> "The leader's function is to provide opportunities for teachers to work together in self-managing teams to improve *their own* **instruction**, always with the expectation for improved learning."
>
> *emphasis in original, Schmoker, 2005, p. 147*

Question 2.a.

Newmann & Wehlage (1995) state that "groups, rather than individuals, are seen as the main units" (p. 38) for doing this work. What are the groups that you have in your school? How do they contribute to improvement? Are they the "main unit" for this improvement?

Question 2.b.

What evidence do you have that teachers in your building 1) "participate in reflective dialogue to learn more about professional issues," 2) "observe and react to one another's teaching, curriculum, and assessment practices," and 3) "engage in joint planning and curriculum development" (Newmann & Wehlage, 1995, p. 31) both within your building and in other schools?

Question 2.c.

What incentive systems do you have or could you use to ensure collaboration? If this is not a strength of you or the school, reach out to others to learn what could be done.

CHALLENGE EXERCISE 2.a.

Specialist teachers are those who tend to struggle seeing their "fit" in a collaborative environment. Have an informal conversation with a number of these staff in your building using this prompt, writing down their responses and identifying what you will do differently: What could I do to facilitate your learning with colleagues in getting better at your craft?

CHALLENGE EXERCISE 2.b.

Explore the School Reform Initiative website (https://www.schoolreforminitiative.org/protocols/) (or others) and identify three protocols that you would like to use with your staff in the next few weeks. What are you most excited about?

CHALLENGE EXERCISE 2.c.

Obtain copies of your district's curriculum guides. Engage with teachers in analyzing the content based on Chapter Nine in **Let's Put the C in PLC**, specifically noting levels of Bloom and kinds of targets. Use this work to engage staff in further clarifying student learning targets.

CHALLENGE EXERCISE 2.d.

After completing Challenge Exercise 2.c., use this information to engage in conversations with teams in thinking about the type of evidence they are using to assess student learning, as well as to think about the specific assessment tool being used. What alignment and/or mismatches do you see?

CHALLENGE EXERCISE 2.e.

Complete the following chart by identifying the data sources that your school currently uses to make decisions about improvement efforts.

Achievement Data	Program Data

Demographic Data	Perception Data

If there are subject areas where you don't have data, why not? Where can you go to find more high-quality data?

Question 2.d.

Study the Data Boot Camp Knowledge Map. Which items are a challenge for you? Which ones do you know already?

CHALLENGE EXERCISE 2.f.

Engage a team of teachers in the lesson study process. What worked? What was a struggle? What will you be sure to do/not do the next time you do this work with a team?

CHALLENGE EXERCISE 2.g.

Engage a teacher in the process of having them videotape their instruction, watching it, and then reflecting with you and/or a colleague on what they saw and what they want to improve. Be sure to remain non-judgmental in your engagement with them. Then reflect: How did it go? What did you learn? What did the teachers learn?

Question 2.e.

What PLC model do you use? What are the key elements of the process? What might be some ways that the process could be strengthened?

CHALLENGE EXERCISE 2.h.

Explore the resource from the Washington State ASCD affiliate (http://wsascd.org/wp-content/uploads/Article_Virtual-Engagement-Strategies.pdf). Identify three new tools and how you will use them in the next few weeks. Which ones are you most excited about?

Question 2.f.

Trang utilized a number of aspects of the learning from this chapter. Reread her story. What new insights emerge for you? How might you put those insights into practice, including in a Remote Learning environment? What resources will you need to make that happen? What obstacles do you anticipate and how might you overcome them?

NOTES AND REFLECTIONS

CHAPTER THREE
STAFF MEETINGS

Elements of Principal Knowledge in Creating a Collaborative Workplace Environment for Teachers

To build a collaborative culture of professional learning, principals know and understand that:

3. **Staff meetings should focus on learning and improvement**
    A. Reduce or remove "adminis-trivia" from staff meetings
    B. Lambert's Tenets of Leadership

Question 3.a.

Reflect on your staff meetings (including those that are remote). To what extent are these meetings focused on the learning of staff that will improve their practice and results for students? What are some actions that you might take to shift the function of these meetings more to adult learning needs?

CHALLENGE EXERCISE 3.a.

Identify agenda items from an upcoming meeting that could be done in another way (memo, email, conversations, etc.). Make a plan to have these agenda items done in that way, and then follow through on that plan. After implementation, what went well? What did you like about this method? What kind of feedback did you receive from staff?

CHALLENGE EXERCISE 3.b.

If you don't already have one, create a template memo to use for sending "admin-is-trivia" to staff. If you do already have one, ask principal colleagues what they use. Share with each other and make revisions based on what you are learning.

CHALLENGE EXERCISE 3.c.

Using Chart One (p. 54) in the book, answer the reflective questions on p. 53. Share your thinking with principal colleagues.

1. Which of these tenets am I most skillful in implementing?

2. Which of these tenets do I need to develop?

3. How might I go about developing this Knowledge/Skill?

4. How will I know that I've been successful in developing this Knowledge/Skill?

Question 3.b.

Lenny utilized a number of aspects of the learning from this chapter. Reread his story. What new insights emerge for you? How might you put those insights into practice? What resources will you need to make that happen? What obstacles do you anticipate and how might you overcome them?

NOTES AND REFLECTIONS

CHAPTER FOUR
PRINCIPLES OF ADULT LEARNING

Elements of Principal Knowledge in Creating a Collaborative Workplace Environment for Teachers

To build a collaborative culture of professional learning, principals know and understand:

4. **Principles of adult learning**
    A. External trainings are of limited usefulness because the challenge is to implement what is already known
    B. Characteristics of a Knowledge Worker
        1. Autonomy, complexity, and a connection between effort and reward
    C. Professional learning designs
        1. Assessment as professional learning
        2. Curriculum as professional learning
        3. Data analysis
        4. Lesson study
        5. Instructional coaching
        6. Professional learning communities
        7. Visual dialogue
    D. Job-embedded professional learning

CHALLENGE EXERCISE 4.a.

Make a list of all the professional development experiences (workshops, trainings, conferences) you have gone to in the last three to five years. Then identify the specific changes you have made to your practice based on that learning.

PD Experience	Time in Training	Changes to Your Practice

What do you notice about this activity? Engage others in a similar activity and reflect on what this might mean for both your own learning and leading the learning of your staff.

> **"Teachers do not learn best from outside experts or by attending conferences or implementing 'programs' installed by outsiders. Teachers learn best from other teachers, in settings where they literally teach each other the art of teaching."**
>
> *Schmoker, 2005, p. 141*

CHALLENGE EXERCISE 4.b.

Make a list of all the job-embedded professional learning (walkthroughs, conversations, book studies, collaborative learning walks, PD planning, curriculum or assessment development, instructional design, teaching others what you have learned, etc.), in which you have engaged in the last three to five years. Then identify the specific changes you have made to your practice based on that learning.

PD Experience	Time in Training	Changes to Your Practice

What do you notice about this activity? Engage others in a similar activity and reflect on what this might mean for both your own learning and leading the learning of your staff.

Question 4.a.

Pfeffer and Sutton state that success "depends largely on implementing what is already known rather than from adopting new or previously unknown ways of doing things." Take some time to identify practices that you know you should do, but don't. This could be things that you don't have the time to do, or lack the confidence, or need a partner, or other reasons. Be brutally honest in identifying your gaps. Then, after identifying your gaps and potential reasons for those gaps, think about what actions you might take to overcome those obstacles and close the Knowing-Doing Gap.

Gaps in Practice	Possible Reasons	Actions to Close the Gap

Question 4.b.

Consider the implications of autonomy, as presented in the book. To what extent do you set a culture of autonomy within an interdependent culture in your building? How effective are you in doing this? How do you know?

Question 4.c.

Consider the implications of complexity, as presented in the book. (p. 64 – 65) To what extent do you create a culture of innovativeness, as distinct from innovation, in your building? How effective are you in doing this? How do you know?

Question 4.d.

Consider the implications of the connection between effort and reward, as presented in the book. To what extent do your staff see this connection in your building? How effective are you in doing this? How do you know?

Question 4.e.

Consider the story from the large vehicle air conditioning plant. What connections do you make to your own practice? How would staff from your building reply to this thinking?

CHALLENGE EXERCISE 4.c.

Explore the websites presented in the book (p. 64 – 65) and identify three resources that you will use in the next few weeks. Which ones are you most excited about?

Question 4.f.

Keisha utilized a number of aspects of the learning from this chapter. Reread her story. What new insights emerge for you? How might you put those insights into practice? What resources will you need to make that happen? What obstacles do you anticipate and how might you overcome them?

CHALLENGE EXERCISE 4.d.

Explore the Innovation Configuration Maps presented in the book (or find others online). With a team of teachers, create your own IC Map based on a change that the school is leading. Get feedback from staff and use it as a tool to inform professional learning and next steps.

NOTES AND REFLECTIONS

CHAPTER FIVE
CONTINUOUS IMPROVEMENT AND INNOVATION

Elements of Principal Knowledge in Creating a Collaborative Workplace Environment for Teachers

To build a collaborative culture of professional learning, principals know and understand that:

5. Continuous improvement is necessary. Effective elements include:
    A. Focusing resources on a small number of goals
    B. Data collection and analysis
    C. The use of multiple sources to guide and demonstrate improvement
    D. Research-based decision-making
    E. A simple focus on refining processes in small ways
    F. Clear, frequent talk about instruction
    G. Recognition and celebration for superior practices and results
    H. Inventiveness/innovativeness where risk-taking is encouraged
    I. High expectations for learning
    J. Using groups as the main units for improvement

Question 5.a.

Consider the seeming dichotomy of continuous improvement and innovation. What are the elements of continuous improvement that you currently use? What aspects of creating a culture of innovativeness do you have in place? How do you know that the two are working?

Question 5.b.

To what extent do you and your organization focus on the learning of individuals within the system—not just students, but also staff?

Question 5.c.

Reflect on the goal(s) of your school. How many are there? How lofty or stretch worthy are they? How was data used to identify them? What data was used to identify them? How was professional expertise honored in the setting of them? How is data used to monitor, assess, and evaluate the school's impact on them?

CHALLENGE EXERCISE 5.a.

Reread the types of data shared in the book. Go back to CHALLENGE EXERCISE 2.d. in this action guide and think about that work through the lens of the goal(s) that you have set. What revisions might you need to make to your data usage processes? What steps do you need to take to ensure that this happens?

Question 5.d.

Reflect on the extent that the existence of one or more goals in your building is changing the behavior of adults to improve their practice. To what extent is your goal(s) a good goal? What evidence do you have to support this assertion? What could be done to strengthen the goal(s) to improve effectiveness and results for students?

CHALLENGE EXERCISE 5.b.

Reflect on the resources that are currently allocated toward the attainment of the goal(s) in your organization. Is it adequate to make a difference in adult practice and student learning? If not, what can be done to make it so? Use the following chart to assist you.

Goal(s)	Current Resources	Potential Changes

In addition to those detailed in Chapter Seven, a sampling of available resources might include:

- Written action plan based on a comprehensive analysis of data (a profile)
- Research- or evidence-based interventions
- A mindset of simple improvements over time
- Methods for monitoring, assessing, and evaluating the impact of interventions
- Ongoing data collection that is made public for monitoring, assessing, and evaluating the impact of interventions
- Allocated time for you to
  - Get in classrooms
  - Talk about instruction
  - Learn about quality curriculum, instruction, and assessment practices
  - Recognize and celebrate the quality and improvement of instruction
- A culture where risk-taking is encouraged and expected
- Small groups of staff working to implement professional learning

Question 5.e.

What intervention(s) is/are your school using to improve adults' practice and results for students? What research or evidence is there that they will actually work?

CHALLENGE EXERCISE 5.c.

Review the resources that are highlighted in this chapter. Choose two or three that you would like to learn more about and spend some time researching them. Then engage in dialogue with colleagues about what research- or evidence-based interventions they are using and how you could strengthen the work of your school to get better.

Question 5.f.

What evidence can you point to that would show that your school is focusing on "small but innumerable and incremental" improvements?

CHALLENGE EXERCISE 5.d.

Choose a week and track when you are in classrooms, how much time you are in them, what classrooms you are spending time in, and for what reason.

Day	Time	Total Time in Room	Classroom	Why You Were There

What do you notice? What strategies might you use to address the patterns that you see emerging?

CHALLENGE EXERCISE 5.e.

Choose some of the teachers from exercise 5.d. and engage in a conversation with them about what you saw, heard, and/or felt. Remember and utilize the strategies from Chapter One. After having these conversations, what did you learn about yourself? About them? About instruction? About the school?

Question 5.g.

What are the celebrations and rituals that your school uses to create and establish a culture of instructional improvement? How often are they? Who is involved in them? How might you leverage these celebrations for continued success?

Question 5.h.

What are some strategies and actions that you use to ensure a climate of innovativeness and reduce a sense of innovation fatigue? (HINT: A culture of innovativeness comes from the staff—bottom-up, whereas innovation fatigue generally comes from top-down initiatives.)

Question 5.i.

What is your school's instructional framework? If you don't have one, what steps might you take to create or establish one? If you do have one, how well is it being used? How do you know? How might you strengthen its usage to increase talk about instruction and improve the practice of adults?

Question 5.j.

Juan utilized a number of aspects of the learning from this chapter. Reread his story. What new insights emerge for you? How might you put those insights into practice? What might you need to make that happen? What obstacles do you anticipate and how might you overcome them?

Question 5.k.

Reflect on the story of Juan and each of the elements of continuous improvement, then consider your own school. In what ways does your school go about meeting each element?

1. Focusing resources on a small number of goals

2. Data collection and analysis

3. The use of multiple sources to guide and demonstrate improvement

4. Research-based decision-making

5. A simple focus on refining processes in small ways

6. Clear, frequent talk about instruction

7. Recognition and celebration for superior practices and results

8. Inventiveness/innovativeness where risk-taking is encouraged

9. High expectations for learning

10. Using groups as the main units for improvement

NOTES AND REFLECTIONS

CHAPTER SIX

MODEL LEARNING

Elements of Principal Knowledge in Creating a Collaborative Workplace Environment for Teachers

To build a collaborative culture of professional learning, principals know and understand that they must:

6. Model professional learning by participating in administrator learning communities
   A. Default mode: Learning
   B. Leadership vs. Management

Question 6.a.

Think about your conversations with staff in the last week or longer. How many of them were directives? What could you have said or done differently to change those interactions so that they were "about seeking answers and asking questions"?

CHALLENGE EXERCISE 6.a.

Reflect on your interactions with staff using the following scales:

On a scale of 1 to 10, how directive vs inquiry-driven do you think you are?

1   2   3   4   5   6   7   8   9   10

Directive   Inquiry Driven

On a scale of 1 to 10, how clearly do you communicate to others (both verbally and nonverbally) that you are open to your own learning and improvement?

1   2   3   4   5   6   7   8   9   10

I Know What I Need to Know   I Am Always Learning and Improving and
                                       Want to Know More and Get Better

Ask your teacher colleagues to use the same scales and anonymously reflect on their interactions with you. Additionally, ask them to identify actions that you could take to move along the continuum. Collect that data and compare it to your own self-assessment. What do you notice? What actions did they suggest that might be helpful?

CHALLENGE EXERCISE 6.b.

Reflect on your approach to life and service. Self-assess on the following scale: How humble are you?

On a scale of 1 to 10, how humble do you think you are?

1	2	3	4	5	6	7	8	9	10
Arrogant									Humble

Ask your teacher colleagues to use the same scale and anonymously rate you. Additionally, ask them to share evidence and identify actions that you take that support their rating of you. Collect that data and compare it to your own self-assessment. What do you notice? What actions might you consider to increase both your humility and the perception that others have of your humility?

Question 6.b.

Reflect on times when directives ARE necessary. Identify those, and strive to limit your directives to these situations.

Question 6.c.

Reflect on the time you allocate for leadership (meeting the needs of everyone) and management (meeting the needs of individuals) roles. What factors are you using to distinguish between the two? What are some of the reasons that you have for being clear about the distinction between the two? How can you be sure that you are able to prioritize leadership activities?

CHALLENGE EXERCISE 6.c.

Reflect on how you allocate your time. How much do you invest in leadership? How much do you spend on management? Have a conversation with principal colleagues about this. In particular, discuss strategies that you and they use to maximize leadership while ensuring effective management in the least amount of time.

Question 6.d.

Think of one or more staff members who might need to be brought "back to life as a learner." How might you "be inventive, persistent, and hold high expectations" in your pursuit to do this? Consider the role of relationships, professional development, peer mentoring, and the establishment and support of schoolwide learning communities.

Question 6.e.

How much time per week do you spend on your own professional learning? What principal colleagues do you spend time with in improving your own practice (e.g., talking about instruction, examining teacher practice, using data, etc.)? How might you go about increasing this investment in yourself and your school?

Question 6.f.

Think about the language that you use regarding learning. To what extent do you use phrases like those shared in the book ("One of the strategies we're learning about is..." or "Something you might consider is..." or "Some of our colleagues learned about...")? How might you go about increasing your use of this type of language of learning?

Question 6.g.

Natalia utilized a number of aspects of the learning from this chapter. Reread her story. What new insights emerge for you? How might you put those insights into practice? What might you need to make that happen? What obstacles do you anticipate and how might you overcome them?

CHALLENGE EXERCISE 6.d.

Take some time to explore the website of the professional organizations listed in the book (and others). Bookmark or otherwise make note of those resources that you would like to spend time exploring on your own and/or with others. Make a plan for how and when you will do that exploration. As you are digging into those resources, consider how you implement your learning, as well as how you will know that the implementation is successful in improving your practice and creating a collaborative culture in your school.

Website	Resource/Link	Who you will use it with	When you will use it	How you will use it
www.ascd.org				
www.learningforward.org				

Website	Resource/Link	Who you will use it with	When you will use it	How you will use it
www.pdkintl.org				
www.naesp.org				
www.nassp.org				

NOTES AND REFLECTIONS

CHAPTER SEVEN
ALLOCATE RESOURCES

Elements of Principal Knowledge in Creating a Collaborative Workplace Environment for Teachers

To build a collaborative culture of professional learning, principals know and understand that:

7. Resources should be allocated to improve student learning
    A. Tangible resources
        1. Time
        2. Materials
        3. Equipment
        4. Space
    B. Intangible resources
        1. Training on protocols and procedures
        2. Administrative support
        3. Trust between teachers
        4. Access to new ideas and expertise

Question 7.a.

The book identifies a variety of resources that are both tangible and intangible. What surprised you about this list? Why or why not?

Question 7.b.

Think about the resources identified by Learning Forward. What specific resources do you allocate and/or focus for each of these items?

- Allocates resources to support job-embedded professional development in the school

- Focuses resources on a small number of high-priority goals

- Allocates resources to provide for continuous improvement of school staff

- Allocates resources so technology supports student learning

Question 7.c.

Consider the resources identified by the National Association of Elementary School Principals. What do you currently do to ensure each of these? What steps might you take to increase your investment in these resources?

- Provide time for reflection as an important part of improving practice

- Invest in teacher learning

- Connect professional development to school learning goals

- Provide opportunities for teachers to work, plan, and think together

- Recognize the need to continually improve principals' own professional practice

CHALLENGE EXERCISE 7.a.

The book discusses the tangible resources of time, materials, equipment, and space. Identify, specifically, the resources you allocate for each of these. Then reflect on what changes might need to be made to ensure that resources are invested where greater collaboration will result. Finally, share your reflections with colleagues (teacher and/or principal colleagues) and talk about specific next steps.

Resource	Current Investments	Possible Changes
Time		
Materials		
Equipment		
Space		

CHALLENGE EXERCISE 7.b.

I've yet to meet a leader who says that they have all the time they need for staff to engage in professional learning; time is our most precious commodity. Download and review the "Establishing Time for Professional Learning" guide referenced in the book. Identify three to five ways that you could re-allocate time in your building. Engage in a conversation with your staff and/or principal colleagues to consider next steps.

CHALLENGE EXERCISE 7.c.

The book also discusses the intangible resources of training on protocols and procedures, administrative support, trust between teachers, and access to new ideas and expertise. Identify, specifically, the resources you allocate for each of these. Then reflect on what changes might need to be made to ensure that resources are invested where greater collaboration will result. Finally, share your reflections with colleagues (teacher and/or principal colleagues) and talk about specific next steps.

Resource	Current Investments	Possible Changes
Training on protocols and procedures		
Administrative support		
Trust between teachers		
Access to new ideas and expertise		

Question 7.d.

What are some of the materials staff have requested for their professional learning? To what extent have these aligned with School Improvement priorities? What actions might you take to assist staff in understanding those priorities and therefore better aligning their requests with them?

CHALLENGE EXERCISE 7.d.

Go back to CHALLENGE EXERCISE 6.d. Create a plan for how you will visit at least one of these (and/or other) sites each week to stay abreast of current resources that may be helpful to staff.

Question 7.e.

Consider the additional resources discussed in the book. Which of these might be helpful to you and/or your staff. How might you go about acquiring these?

Question 7.f.

On a scale of 1 to 10, how trusting of an environment do you perceive there to be between teachers?

| 1 | 2 | 3 | 4 | 5 | 6 | 7 | 8 | 9 | 10 |

Not at All   Highly Trusting

How do you know? What steps might you take to build trust in the building?

CHALLENGE EXERCISE 7.e.

At an upcoming meeting, get out your cell phone and set a timer. Unobtrusively make note on a sheet of scratch paper who in the room talks, as well as for how long. In light of the Google study, what does this say to you? What steps do you need to take based on this data? Repeat this exercise for the same group later, and with other groups. What are you learning through this exercise?

CHALLENGE EXERCISE 7.f.

At an upcoming meeting, notice the nonverbal cues that people in the room give each other. What are you noticing? What actions might you take? Remember that the point of this is to build trust and psychological safety so that the group can be as effective as possible—to put the C in PLC!

CHALLENGE EXERCISE 7.g.

Take some time to look at the protocols at the School Reform Initiative (https://www.schoolreforminitiative.org/protocols) or elsewhere. Identify at least one protocol that you would like to use with one particular group in order to enhance their turn-taking skills.

Question 7.g.

What are the procedures that you have in place to facilitate processes in your building? Consider those areas identified in the book, as well as others. What clarifications might you make to enhance the effectiveness and efficiency of these procedures?

CHALLENGE EXERCISE 7.h.

Take your list of procedures from the previous question and share these with a principal colleagues. Engage in a conversation with them, sharing your thinking and getting ideas from them. Make revisions to your procedures as appropriate.

CHALLENGE EXERCISE 7.i.

Think about an upcoming staff meeting. What parts of that meeting could be put into a memo? Do it. Share the memo with some teacher and principal colleagues to gather their feedback on this first one. Make this practice a regular part of your work.

CHALLENGE EXERCISE 7.j.

Ask your teachers what administrative duties they are required to do that have minimal or no impact on student learning. Compile this list and use it to consider what can be removed from their plates to increase effectiveness and efficiency.

Question 7.h.

Consider the opportunities that you provide your staff to access new ideas and expertise. What are those opportunities? When and how often are they? How many of your staff access them? What are the results from these? What evidence do you have that those results are impacting educator practice and results for students?

Question 7.i.

Reread Karyn's story. What new insights emerge for you? How might you put those insights into practice? What resources will you need to make that happen?

NOTES AND REFLECTIONS

CHAPTER EIGHT
INVOLVE STAFF

Elements of Principal Knowledge in Creating a Collaborative Workplace Environment for Teachers

To build a collaborative culture of professional learning, principals know and understand that:

8. Staff should be involved in important decisions
   A. The use of a leadership team
   B. Opportunity for input is provided, encouraged, expected, implemented

Question 8.a.

Reflect on your leadership style using the following scale:

On a scale of 1 to 10, how micromanaging vs. empowering do you think you are?

1	2	3	4	5	6	7	8	9	10
Micromanaging									Empowering

What evidence do you have to support your rating?

CHALLENGE EXERCISE 8.a.

Ask your teacher colleagues to anonymously rate you on the above scale. Write down common themes that emerge for you, then use this information to inform your thinking and actions in the rest of this chapter.

Question 8.b.

Reflect on the degree to which "opportunities for input from all staff are provided, encouraged, expected, and implemented." Consider each aspect of the statement using a 1 to 10 scale:

- **Opportunities for input from all staff are** *provided*
- **Opportunities for input from all staff are** *encouraged*
- **Opportunities for input from all staff are** *expected*
- **Opportunities for input from all staff are** *implemented*

What steps might you take to increase these opportunities. How will you know that you have been successful?

Question 8.c.

What "core leadership group" do you have in your school? What groups are represented on it? To what extent does this group take responsibility for initiating and sustaining an ongoing conversation of school change? What might you do to increase the use and relevancy of this group?

CHALLENGE EXERCISE 8.b.

What is your philosophy of leadership? Consider Lambert's tenets (and other resources) to inform your thinking. Write it down. Share it with others (teachers, principals, central office leaders, friends, etc.). Gather their feedback. Make revisions to it. Then, use it as a touchstone to make decisions and guide your actions.

Question 8.d.

Think of times when leadership has emerged in unwanted ways in your organization. What are some steps that could have been taken to distribute leadership proactively (and positively)? What can you learn from those situations and apply to your current or future leadership challenges?

Question 8.e.

Reflect on times when leadership was proactively and positively distributed. What qualities or circumstances defined those situations? What can you learn from these and apply to your current or future leadership challenges?

CHALLENGE EXERCISE 8.c.

Access a list of all of your staff. Given that all instructional staff must be involved in the work of leadership, go through your list and identify the specific ways that each staff member is engaged in this work. For any staff members who are not currently involved, identify ways that you could meaningfully engage them. Talk with principal colleagues about this work to get ideas and feedback.

Question 8.f.

Think about the ways that you build leadership skills and capacity of the entire staff. What are the skills you are building? Who, when, and how are you building them? How do you know that you are being successful?

Skills	Who, When, and How you are building them	Measures of success

Skills	Who, When, and How you are building them	Measures of success

Question 8.g.

Reflect on recent decisions made by a core leadership team. What specific steps did you take to empower the follow-through of those decisions?

CHALLENGE EXERCISE 8.d.

Make a list of upcoming decisions that will need to be made for the school. Who will make them? How will the decisions be made? How will they be implemented? How will you know that implementation is successful?

Upcoming decision	Who makes it?	How to make it	How to implement it	What you will watch for to decide success?

Question 8.h.

Refer to the five-step plan from Marzano et al. (2005). Which of these steps have you taken? Which ones do you need to strengthen? How might you go about doing that? What do you need to learn about in order to lead this work?

1. Develop a strong school leadership team.
2. Distribute some responsibilities throughout the leadership team.
3. Select the right work.
4. Identify the order of magnitude implied by the selected work.
5. Match the management style to the order of magnitude of the change initiative.

CHALLENGE EXERCISE 8.e.

Using Covey's quadrants, identify those specific activities in which you lead and/or engage by quadrant based on an ideal situation. Then make note of how you actually spend your time. What do you notice? What steps might you take to better align the ideal with the reality?

The Time Management Matrix

	Urgent	Not Urgent
Important	I	II
Not Important	III	IV

Question 8.i.

Using Chart 5 (p. 119) in *Let's Put the C in PLC*, consider the structures that you have in place to engage all staff in the work of improvement. What changes might you need to make in order to better engage all staff, as well as align priorities toward desired results?

Question 8.j.

Jai utilized a number of aspects of the learning from this chapter. Reread the story. What new insights emerge for you? How might you put those insights into practice? What might you need to make that happen? What obstacles do you anticipate and how might you overcome them?

NOTES AND REFLECTIONS

CHAPTER NINE
PRINCIPLES OF STUDENT LEARNING

Elements of Principal Knowledge in Creating a Collaborative Workplace Environment for Teachers

To build a collaborative culture of professional learning, principals know and understand:

9. Aspects of student learning
    A. Curriculum
        1. What students should learn
        2. Alignment of daily objectives with grade-level outcomes to program goals
        3. A variety of Bloom's taxonomy verbs
        4. A variety of Kinds of Targets (KRiSP)
    B. Instruction
        1. Content and Pacing
            a. Daily lessons match curricular expectations
            b. Appropriate instructional level
            c. Pacing appropriate to maintain engagement
        2. Climate
            a. Appropriate discipline for orderly environment
            b. High expectations
            c. Efficient allocation of time
            d. Students on task and participating actively
            e. Structure for daily routines
            f. Many instructional strategies/tools
            g. Instructional strategies/tools matched to learning target(s)
    C. Assessment
        1. Students' involved in assessment process
        2. Alignment between EWATR (Expectations, Written curriculum, Assessments, Taught curriculum, and what is Reported)
        3. Type of Evidence matches Kind of Target

a. Teacher Observation: Knowledge, Reasoning, or Skill-level targets
b. Selected Response: Knowledge-level targets
c. Extended Written Response: Knowledge, Reasoning, or Product-level targets
d. Performance Tasks: Reasoning, Skill, and Product-level targets

Question 9.a.

"Principals in PLCs are called upon to regard themselves as leaders of leaders rather than leaders of followers, and broadening teacher leadership becomes one of their priorities" (DuFour et al, 2005, p. 23). It is impossible for you to be a subject-matter expert in every curricular area. What areas of expertise (non-curricular) do you have that you can leverage as a leader of leaders?

Question 9.b.

How do you and your colleagues (teacher and principal) define the word "curriculum"? How can you clarify and come to a common understanding of this definition with others? What processes does your school use to create, revise, access, and store your curriculum?

CHALLENGE EXERCISE 9.a.

Before we get into thinking about the school's philosophy and beliefs, spend some time thinking about your own. Write down what you believe about:

1. The Process of Leadership

2. Leaders as People

3. The Role of Leaders

4. The Importance of Leadership

Share this document with others to gather their feedback. Make revisions to it. Use it as a touchstone to guide your leadership.

CHALLENGE EXERCISE 9.b.

In what programs and/or content areas has your school clarified its philosophy and beliefs? If you have these, in what ways are these used to guide decision-making? If you do not have them, use the process outlined in the book to create them. What are you learning about yourself and the organization through this process of having and/or clarifying beliefs?

CHALLENGE EXERCISE 9.c.

In what programs and/or content areas has your school identified program goals? If you have these, in what ways are these used to guide decision-making? If you do not have them, use a process to create them (you could replicate the process from philosophy and beliefs). What are you learning about yourself and the organization through this process of having and/or clarifying program goals?

CHALLENGE EXERCISE 9.d.

Obtain a copy of your district's curriculum guide. If it doesn't have one, reach out to principal colleagues in other districts to get one. With teacher colleagues, go through the **essential outcomes, questions, or standards** (depending on what they are called) and identify the level of rigor for each one, based on Bloom's Taxonomy. Engage in a conversation with your teacher colleagues: What do you notice? How aligned are these with the program goals? What needs to be changed or revised? How might we go about making these revisions? What obstacles stand in our way? What resources would be helpful to accomplish these changes to your curriculum?

CHALLENGE EXERCISE 9.e.

Using the same curriculum guide, with teacher colleagues, go through the **objectives, indicators, or key concepts** (depending on what they are called) and identify the level of rigor for each one, based on Bloom's Taxonomy. Engage in a conversation with your teacher colleagues: What do you notice? How aligned are these daily targets with the larger essential standards or questions? What needs to be changed or revised? How might we go about making these revisions? What obstacles stand in our way? What resources would be helpful to accomplish these changes to your curriculum?

CHALLENGE EXERCISE 9.f.

Reflect on the extent of conversations around instructional practices in your building—specifically, questions three and four of the PLC process: What will we do when students don't know or are not able to do it, and What will we do if they already know or can do it? Self-assess on the following scales.

On a scale of 1 to 10, to what extent are instructional conversations prevalent in your organization?

1	2	3	4	5	6	7	8	9	10
Never									All the Time

On a scale of 1 to 10, how would you rate the quality of the instructional conversations in your organization?

1	2	3	4	5	6	7	8	9	10
Poor									Incredible

Ask your teacher colleagues to use the same scale to rate their perception. Additionally, ask them to share evidence and identify actions that support their rating. Collect that data and compare it to your own self-assessment. What do you notice? What actions might you consider to increase the frequency and quality of instructional conversations? What barriers do you currently face, and what might be potential roadblocks in the future? How might you overcome these?

CHALLENGE EXERCISE 9.g.

If your district has an instructional framework, get it and use it for the remaining exercises in this chapter. Before proceeding, compare what you find in your instructional framework to what is presented in this chapter as it relates to 1) Lesson content and pace, 2) Climate, and 3) Assessment. What overlaps or gaps do you notice? What similarities do you find?

If your district does not have an instructional framework, use the elements described as an overarching way of thinking about instruction in your school. What do you notice about what is described and how instruction plays out in your building?

CHALLENGE EXERCISE 9.h.

Using the curriculum guide used previously as a lens through which to observe instruction, engage in some classroom observations with teacher and/or principal colleagues. Thinking about lesson content and pace, what are you noticing in terms of

1) Content alignment and appropriateness

2) Understandability—clarity of what students are learning and how it is taught

3) Pacing—not too fast and not too slow

What conclusions can you draw about these three areas? What evidence supports your conclusions? Engage in role-play with a colleague around these ideas, then engage in this dialogue with the teacher(s) that you observed. Reflect on the impact of these conversations—on you, the other person(s), and the school.

CHALLENGE EXERCISE 9.i.

Now engage in some classroom observations with teacher and/or principal colleagues focused on the classroom climate. What are you noticing in terms of

1) Appropriate discipline

2) High expectations

3) Efficient allocation of time

4) Students on task and participating actively

5) Structure for classroom work

6) Use of instructional strategies

What conclusions can you draw about these six areas? What evidence supports your conclusions? Engage in a mock conversation with a colleague around these ideas, then engage in this dialogue with the teacher(s) that you observed. Reflect on the impact of these conversations—on you, the other person(s), and the school.

Question 9.c.

Reflect on the overall use of time in your school. What are some disruptions that are caused by and/or endorsed (formally or informally) by you and/or the office? How might these be reduced or eliminated?

Question 9.d.

Think about teachers in your building. Which ones are particularly strong in either 1) Lesson content and pacing or 2) Climate? How might you and the school leverage the strengths of these teachers to spread these strengths to others? What obstacles stand in the way? What resources are necessary to overcome these obstacles? How will you know that you have been successful or are on the right path?

Question 9.e.

Thinking about the aspects of 1) Lesson content and pace and 2) Climate, which ones might there be a common language on the staff? How might you leverage this common language to create a culture of talk about instruction? Where might you need to work to increase this common language?

CHALLENGE EXERCISE 9.j.

Explore resources that you have around instructional practices (possibly including those in the Wanting More? section of the book). Engage in dialogue with colleagues about what you are reading. Consider what elements can be pulled out and emphasized as part of creating a collaborative culture focused on improving instructional practices.

Question 9.f.

Consider the assessment practices in your building. On a scale of 1 to 10, how would you rate the extent to which assessment is considered a powerful tool for improving professional practice and student learning?

1 2 3 4 5 6 7 8 9 10

Assessment For Compliance   Assessment As Improvement

What evidence do you have to support this rating? What steps might you consider to move the school along the continuum?

Question 9.g.

Rate the extent of the use of assessment information on the following scale:

1 2 3 4 5 6 7 8 9 10

Assessment of Learning   Assessment for Learning

What evidence do you have to support this rating? What steps might you consider to move the school along the continuum? Consider, especially, the involvement of students in the assessment process.

CHALLENGE EXERCISE 9.k.

Engage in a conversation with teacher colleagues about their assessment practices. First examine specific assessment tools for alignment between what is Expected, Written, Assessed, and Taught. What do you notice? What do the teachers notice? What revisions need to be made? Further, examine these tools for:

1. Clarity of targets

2. Appropriateness of the assessment tools

3. Usefulness of reporting

CHALLENGE EXERCISE 9.l.

With the same assessment tools examined above, and with the same colleagues, use the resources provided in the book to identify the Kind of Target (KRiSP) and evaluate the Type of Evidence (Teacher Observation, Selected Response, Extended Written Response, and Performance Assessment). What do you notice about this alignment? What changes need to be made?

CHALLENGE EXERCISE 9.m.

Engage in conversation with your teacher colleagues: To what extent are the clear learning targets driving instruction? What steps could be taken to increase this? What obstacles might be in the way? What resources could be accessed to overcome these?

CHALLENGE EXERCISE 9.n.

Obtain a copy of at least one selected response assessment used in your school. Examine it against the targets that are purportedly being measured and determine the appropriateness of this tool based on the KRiSP status of those learning targets. Engage in conversations with teacher colleagues about what you found and what they notice, and consider next steps to ensure high levels of alignment between the Kind of Target and Type of Evidence.

CHALLENGE EXERCISE 9.o.

Identify with teacher colleagues what staff are to know and be able to do as part of the school improvement goal(s). KRiSP these learning targets. Then select the Type(s) of Evidence you will use to measure staff attainment of these learning targets, as well as develop tool(s) that will be used to gather this information. Use these tools to monitor and assess changes in practice toward the attainment of the school improvement goal(s).

CHALLENGE EXERCISE 9.p.

Engage with staff to self-assess their assessment practices by having them reflect on the frequency of assessment tools that they use, based on the Types of Evidence. What do you/they notice? What steps might be taken to better align the Kinds of Targets with Types of Evidence? How and when will this happen?

	Teacher Observation	Selected Response	Extended Written Response	Performance Task
Tools used				

CHALLENGE EXERCISE 9.q.

Based on the tools identified in the previous CHALLENGE EXERCISE, and using the "Links Among Kinds of Targets and Types of Evidence" provided in the book, engage staff in an examination of one or more assessment tools to determine the appropriateness of that tool. What changes need to be made? How can this learning be applied to all assessment tasks? What long-term changes need to be made in the school to ensure tighter alignment between Kinds of Targets and Types of Evidence?

Question 9.h.

Consider the extent to which students understand what they are learning. What steps might be taken to increase this? How will you know that it is successful? Specifically, consider these questions:

Does the student understand what they are learning, each and every day?

Does the assessment and results inform the student?

Does it drive the student's learning?

Are results visible in the classroom?

Can students tell you what they are learning?

NOTES AND REFLECTIONS

CHAPTER TEN
PRINCIPLES OF CHANGE AND SUSTAINABILITY

Elements of Principal Knowledge in Creating a Collaborative Workplace Environment for Teachers

To build a collaborative culture of professional learning, principals know and understand:

10. Principles of change and sustainability
    A. Principles of sustainability
    B. Consensus should be built
    C. Persistence is needed
    D. Meaningful change is extremely hard
    E. There is a difference between adaptive and technical barriers

Question 10.a.

Woodrow Wilson is credited with saying, "If you want to make enemies, try to change something." Reflect on times in your career, either with you or someone else at the helm, where this has been true, and those when it has not been true. What were some of the key differences between them? What can you learn from this and apply to your leadership practices?

Question 10.b.

On the following scale, rate the extent to which you try to control versus lead change:

| 1 | 2 | 3 | 4 | 5 | 6 | 7 | 8 | 9 | 10 |

I Try to Control Change   I Create the Conditions for Change to Occur

What evidence do you have to support this rating? What steps might you consider to move yourself along the continuum? What resources (including people) might you access to be able to do this?

Question 10.c.

Using the following scale, rate the extent to which you exemplify the following qualities:

1   2   3   4   5   6   7   8   9   10

Not at All   This is Who I Am

1. Persistence
2. Inventiveness
3. Holding high expectations
4. Patience
5. Tolerance for ambiguity
6. Attitude of learning and improvement
7. Humility

What evidence do you have to support your ratings? What steps might you consider to move yourself along the continuum? What resources (including people) might you access to be able to do this? How will you know that you are making progress?

Question 10.d.

Identify one change that you are currently leading. What are some of the obstacles you are confronting? Label each as being either technical or adaptive. Then identify specific steps that you can take to overcome these obstacles, including learning that needs to take place for adaptive barriers to be effectively overcome.

Change	Obstacles	Technical or Adaptive?	Learning needed to overcome

CHALLENGE EXERCISE 10.a.

Spend some time on the CBAM website (https://sedl.org/cbam/), and engage in dialogue with colleagues about what you are seeing and learning. What aspects of this model might you use to facilitate your work to lead change? What continued learning do you need to engage in?

Question 10.e.

Reflect on the extent to which you and your school focus on learning first, testing last. To what extent do others agree with your assessment? What steps might you take to ensure that learning is the primary focus, and that this is clear for all stakeholders?

Question 10.f.

Reflect on the extent to which you and your school focus on long-term success. To what extent do others agree with your assessment? What steps might you take to ensure that we are focused on long-term results, and that this is clear for all stakeholders?

Question 10.g.

Reflect on the extent to which you focus on building the leadership capacity of others. What evidence do you have to support your thinking? What steps might you take to ensure that you are building leadership capacity in others?

Question 10.h.

Reflect on the policies or practices of your school or district that exacerbate inequities. What steps might you take to reduce and eliminate these?

Question 10.i.

Reflect on the impact schools can and should have on social justice. In what ways does your organization engage in this work? What steps might you take to advance this principle of sustainability?

CHALLENGE EXERCISE 10.a.

Several questions are raised in the book. Answer them and then engage in conversations with principal and teacher colleagues:

1. How do you ensure that students are thinking of themselves as connected with each other and the planet?

2. How do you empower students to make a difference in their own and others' lives?

3. How do you guarantee that the mistakes of the past don't become replicated in the next generation—that we are, truly, carrying forward an ever-advancing civilization?

4. How do you make sure that the result of learning isn't simply memorization, but a call to the betterment of ourselves and the world around us?

5. What other questions do you need to be asking and attempting to answer?

Question 10.j.

Think about a time when staff changes occurred through retirement or resignations. What changes could have been made to programming or the allocation of human resources to better access the expertise of others (without necessarily rehiring for the position)? Be proactive—what future positions might be shifted in order to maximize effectiveness and results for students?

Question 10.k.

What steps do you take to ensure that the diversity of staff is recognized and valued? Consider diversity of perspectives and practices. What steps might you take to ensure that those voices that have been traditionally marginalized and silenced are instead valued and centered in our thinking and actions?

CHALLENGE EXERCISE 10.b.

Think about how you are proactive with influencing district, state, and federal mandates and guidance. What steps might you take to increase your influence? Make a plan to do it. Share the plan with at least one principal colleague. Ask for their support, and set in motion ways to help hold yourself accountable.

NOTES AND REFLECTIONS

CHAPTER ELEVEN
A CALL TO ACTION

Question 11.a.

Go back through your notes of this workbook. In each chapter, pull out one or two ideas that you need to learn more about in order to become a more effective leader of learning. Write those here.

CHALLENGE EXERCISE 11.a.

Go through your list in the previous question and prioritize them. Then create a plan for how you will go about learning what you need to know to become a more effective leader of learning. Share that plan with one or more principal colleagues. Ask for their support in implementing your plan.

CHALLENGE EXERCISE 11.b.

Now that you have clearly identified what you must know, and created a plan for learning that, identify what you must do differently in order to implement your learning. This may be something that you keep on the forefront of your mind as you go about your learning.

Question 11.b.

Identify obstacles that you might encounter in bridging any potential knowing-doing gap. How might you overcome those? What resources might be helpful in that endeavor?

CHALLENGE EXERCISE 11.c.

Go back through the book and identify stories that were particularly useful for you and checklists that you want to use with yourself and others. Make note of those here so that you can refer back to them regularly.

Now that you know, use this text as a touchstone to come back to and remind yourself of that which you must do. Use the stories to generate additional ways of creating a collaborative community. Use the checklists to self-assess and push yourself further, as well as provide them to others to assess where you and the school are on the journey. Take action. Turn that knowledge into results—for both staff and students.

Write down your reflections, and possibly even share your experiences in story form. Tell the story of how your school is getting better. Share the credit with all involved. As you take action, you will learn through your doing.

APPENDIX

To build a collaborative culture of professional learning, principals need to know and understand these important principles.

1. Charismatic leadership is not necessary for long-term success
    A. Relationships ARE necessary for long-term success
    B. Personal Clarity
    C. Dialogue
    D. Rapport
    E. Pause
    F. Paraphrase
    G. Prompt

2. Teachers should work in teams. Effective elements include:
    A. Effective grouping
    B. A focus on improving instruction/teaching each other by:
        1. Working, planning, and thinking together
        2. Reflecting via dialogue re: professional issues
        3. Observing and reacting to teaching, curriculum, and assessment
        4. Joint lesson planning and curriculum development
    C. The use of protocols
    D. The training of teachers in the skills and knowledge to collaborate
    E. An incentive system
    F. The deprivatization of the classroom
    G. Networking with teachers in other buildings

3. Staff meetings should focus on learning and improvement
    A. Reduce or remove "adminis-trivia" from staff meetings
    B. Lambert's Tenets of Leadership

4. Principles of adult learning
    A. External trainings are of limited usefulness because the challenge is to implement what is already known

B. Characteristics of a Knowledge Worker
   1. Autonomy, complexity, and a connection between effort and reward
C. Professional learning designs
   1. Assessment as professional learning
   2. Curriculum as professional learning
   3. Data analysis
   4. Lesson study
   5. Instructional coaching
   6. Professional learning communities
   7. Visual dialogue
D. Job-embedded professional learning

5. Continuous improvement is necessary. Effective elements include:
   A. Focusing resources on a small number of goals
   B. Data collection and analysis
   C. The use of multiple sources to guide and demonstrate improvement
   D. Research-based decision-making
   E. A simple focus on refining processes in small ways
   F. Clear, frequent talk about instruction
   G. Recognition and celebration for superior practices and results
   H. Inventiveness/innovativeness where risk-taking is encouraged
   I. High expectations for learning
   J. Using groups as the main units for improvement

6. Model professional learning by participating in administrator learning communities
   A. Default mode: Learning
   B. Leadership vs. Management

7. Resources should be allocated to improve student learning
   A. Tangible resources
      1. Time
      2. Materials
      3. Equipment
      4. Space
   B. Intangible resources
      1. Training on protocols and procedures
      2. Administrative support

3. Trust between teachers
4. Access to new ideas and expertise

8. Staff should be involved in important decisions
   A. The use of a leadership team
   B. Opportunity for input is provided, encouraged, expected, implemented

9. Aspects of student learning
   A. Curriculum
      1. What students should learn
      2. Alignment of daily objectives with grade-level outcomes to program goals
      3. A variety of Bloom's taxonomy verbs
      4. A variety of Kinds of Targets (KRiSP)
   B. Instruction
      1. Content and Pacing
         a) Daily lessons match curricular expectations
         b) Appropriate instructional level
         c) Pacing appropriate to maintain engagement
      2. Climate
         a) Appropriate discipline for orderly environment
         b) High expectations
         c) Efficient allocation of time
         d) Students on task and participating actively
         e) Structure for daily routines
         f) Many instructional strategies/tools
         g) Instructional strategies/tools matched to learning target(s)
   C. Assessment
      1. Students' involved in assessment process
      2. Alignment between EWATR (Expectations, Written curriculum, Assessments, Taught curriculum, and what is Reported)
      3. Type of Evidence matches Kind of Target
         a) Teacher Observation: Knowledge, Reasoning, or Skill-level targets
         b) Selected Response: Knowledge-level targets
         c) Extended Written Response: Knowledge, Reasoning, or

      Product-level targets
    d) Performance Tasks: Reasoning, Skill, and Product-level targets

10. Principles of change and sustainability
    A. Principles of sustainability
    B. Consensus should be built
    C. Persistence is needed
    D. Meaningful change is extremely hard
    E. There is a difference between adaptive and technical barriers

ABOUT THE AUTHOR

Dr. Chad Dumas is an educational consultant, international presenter and award-winning researcher whose primary focus is collaborating to develop capacity for continuous improvement. He shares his research and knowledge of how to improve educational outcomes in his new books, *Let's Put the C in PLC* and *An Action Guide to Put the C in PLC*. Having been a successful teacher, principal, central office administrator, professional developer and consultant in a variety of school districts, he brings his passion, knowledge, and skills to his writing and speaking as he engages participants in meaningful and practical learning. By seamlessly weaving engaging stories with education research and offering hands-on tools with clear processes, Chad offers readers and audiences useful knowledge and skills they can implement immediately.

The results of Chad's work speak for themselves. One district was identified as "Persistently Lowest Achieving" upon his arrival, and within a few years — by applying the principles of this book — multiple schools were recognized as National PLC Models for improving student learning. Chad has served on and led accreditation visits for Cognia around the United States and world, presented nationally and internationally, collaborated with school boards, intermediate service agencies, state departments of education, and professional associations, and trained as an agency trainer for Adaptive Schools.

To learn more about Chad's work and to contact him about consulting or speaking, please visit www.NextLearningSolutions.com.

www.ingramcontent.com/pod-product-compliance
Lightning Source LLC
Chambersburg PA
CBHW081507080526
44589CB00017B/2678